Children in our World

~~CANCELLED~~

Poverty AND Hunger

Louise Spilsbury

Hanane Kai

Published in paperback in Great Britain in 2018 by Wayland

Text © Hodder and Stoughton, 2017
Written by Louise Spilsbury
Illustrations © Hanane Kai, 2017

Edited by Corinne Lucas
Designed by Sophie Wilkins

A catalogue for this title is available from the British Library.
ISBN: 978 1 5263 0054 6
10 9 8 7 6 5 4 3 2 1

MIX
Paper from
responsible sources
FSC® C104740
FSC
www.fsc.org

Printed in China

Wayland
An imprint of
Hachette Children's Books
Part of Hodder & Stoughton
Carmelite House
50 Victoria Embankment
London, EC4Y 0DZ

An Hachette UK Company
www.hachette.co.uk
www.hachettechildrens.co.uk

Contents

Most people have enough money to buy the things they need, such as food to be healthy, and lots of the items they want, such as treats.

Poverty means a person has little or no money. They go hungry day after day because they cannot buy enough food to eat. That kind of hunger makes people weak, tired and ill. About one in nine people on Earth do not have enough food to lead a healthy and active life.

The world's poorest families live in developing countries. In these countries most people have very little money. Many people have less than £1.50 a day to buy the food, clean water, clothing, medicine and shelter they need.

There are poor and hungry people in other countries, too. Poverty and hunger are caused by many things, which are often outside of people's control.

Three-quarters of all hungry people rely on farming for their food. The problem is that they may not have enough money to buy land, tools or seeds to grow food. If there is no rain, crops and farm animals might die. Without food to eat, people may starve.

Sometimes people are poor because the business they worked for closed, or they get very low pay for the job they do. Some people have a disability that stops them from working. If the person who makes money for a family leaves, the rest of the family may go hungry.

Wars can make people poor and hungry. During a war people have to fight instead of working to earn money. Farms may be destroyed and farm animals killed. Bombs are sometimes put in fields, which can stop farmers from working on the land for years.

People sometimes have to leave their homes because of war. Refugees are people who escape to a new place where they hope to be safe. But they have no home or job in the new place. That means they cannot earn money to buy food or shelter.

Natural disasters also cause poverty and hunger, and they can happen anywhere. When a flood covers fields with water it destroys the crops so the farmer cannot grow food. Hurricanes destroy houses and shops, leaving people without homes, jobs or food.

The world is getting warmer. Global warming is causing more droughts and other natural disasters. When crops are ruined there is less food to go round. Then, the price of food goes up. This means more people around the world go hungry.

Most people have enough money to pay for a warm, safe home to live in. They have clean water to drink and to wash and cook with. They can afford to buy medicines and pay doctors to help them if they get sick.

Poor people may live in damp or cold houses, or they may have no home at all and sleep on the streets instead. Without a proper home, food or clean water, people may get ill. When they are sick they may not be able to afford doctors or medicines to help them.

Poverty is hard on all children. Some may have to miss out on things such as new clothes and school trips. They may be bullied or teased at school. Can you imagine how this feels? Children do not want to be treated differently just because they are poor.

Some families are too poor to buy the uniforms or books children need to go to school. And some children are too hungry or weak to learn. This makes it hard for them to get a job when they grow up, so their children may also be poor and hungry.

17

A charity is a group that helps families and children in need. In some places, charity workers run food banks. People donate tins and packets of food so poor people can get a box of food from there when they have nothing to eat.

Charities help people to change their lives. In developing countries they give tools to builders or boats to fishing villages so people can work. They help people start a shop or other business. Charities tell people about poverty so they will give money to help people in need.

Charities also help farmers by lending them money to buy tools, machines and seeds for crops. They show farmers how to use fertilizers to make crops grow bigger and better.

When farmers grow lots of healthy crops there is more food to eat or sell. This means the farmer's family has more money. They can spend it on school books, clothes, medicine and other useful things.

We all need clean water to be healthy. In developing countries, charities help people to build wells and pumps so they can get clean water. They help people to build more sinks and toilets. This helps people to avoid disease.

Charities also help people to build hospitals. They teach nurses and doctors, and provide medicine. They make sure babies get the health checks they need. When children grow up healthy they have a better chance of staying healthy as an adult.

It is hard to learn if you are hungry. Imagine going to school with an empty stomach. Hunger makes it difficult to pay attention in class and remember things. Schools can provide free school dinners so children do not go hungry.

People help children in developing countries by building schools and training teachers. This means more children get the chance to learn. When children get an education, it is easier for them to get a better paid job and escape poverty when they grow up.

It is normal to feel sad or angry that some people live in poverty and hunger when other people have so much. If you are upset, talk to an adult about how you feel. They can help you.

Things are getting better all the time. There are fewer poor and hungry people today than there were 20 years ago. That is because people have done things to make a difference and are still helping today.

It feels good to help people. There are lots of things you can do. You could give old toys, books, clothes or other items to a charity shop. You could ask your family to give tins of food to a food bank. You could bake cakes to raise money for a charity that helps people who are poor and hungry around the world. What ideas do you have?

Find Out More

Books

Beatrice's Goat
Page McBrier, Aladdin Paperbacks, 2000

Seeking Refuge: Ali's Story – A Journey from Afghanistan
Andy Glynne, Wayland, 2015

*Who are Refugees and Migrants? What Makes
People Leave their Homes? And Other Big Questions.*
Michael Rosen and Annemarie Young, Wayland, 2016

Websites

Save the Children works to protect children in need all over
the world.
www.savethechildren.org.uk

The Red Cross is a charity that helps victims of war and natural
disasters.
www.redcross.org.uk

UNICEF Kid Power is a charity that gives kids the chance
to help save lives.
https://unicefkidpower.org

Glossary

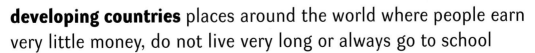

charity a group that helps people in need

crop plants grown for food

developing countries places around the world where people earn very little money, do not live very long or always go to school

disability when someone has a condition that limits what they can do, such as not being able to see or having trouble learning

disease another word for illness

drought when a place gets little or no rain for months or years

fertilizer a substance that helps plants grow bigger and better

flood when water washes on to land and flows through fields, streets and houses causing damage

food bank a place people in need are given food for free

global warming rise in Earth's temperature

hurricane dangerous storm with powerful winds

natural disaster natural events that cause great damage, such as a flood or earthquake

refugee a person who leaves their home country to find a safer place to live because of war or poverty

starve to suffer or die from hunger

Index